WRITES OF THE CHURCH

The Bible Reading Fellowship
15 The Chambers, Vineyard
Abingdon OX14 3FE
brf.org.uk

The Bible Reading Fellowship (BRF) is a Registered Charity (233280)

ISBN 978 0 85746 577 1
First published 2017
10 9 8 7 6 5 4 3 2 1 0
All rights reserved

Text © Gary Alderson 2017
Illustrations © Dave Walker 2017
This edition © The Bible Reading Fellowship 2017

The author asserts the moral right to be identified as the author of this work

A catalogue record for this book is available from the British Library

Printed and bound by CPI Group (UK) Ltd, Croydon CR0 4YY

WRITES OF THE CHURCH

Gripes and grumbles of people in the pews

Gary Alderson

Illustrated by Dave Walker

BRF

CONTENTS

WELCOME

Dear Everyone

At the last Church Council meeting, we agreed that, in this modern age, we need to use social media. People need to stay in touch and share news! And what better way to reach out to a hyper-connected, web-enabled generation?

We discussed Twitter, Facebook, WhatsApp, Instagram, Tumblr and Snapchat.

And then decided to introduce a letters page in the church magazine.

Revd Nathan

9

Dear Sir

The new letters page is a great step forward, but still lacks that face-to-face communication we expect from the church. And when I say the church, I mean of course the vicar.

With 7,000 houses in Tremlett, I have calculated that if the vicar visits ten families a day, he will have covered the whole parish in just two years! He may wear through a few pairs of shoes, but it will be a great step forward.

Constanza Nearby

Dear Sir

If you introduce a letters page to this magazine, people will write stupid, pointless letters complaining unnecessarily.

Bradley Hadleigh

THE PEOPLE

Dear Sir

Over the last year, the vicar has preached on Jesus throwing the money changers out of the temple; Jesus telling the rich young man to give all his money away; and the early church sharing their possessions and helping the poor.

Not once has he mentioned Paul's exhortation that 'God looks after those who look after themselves'.

Faced with this socialism, I resign as church treasurer.

Norbert Dranesqueezer

Dear Sir

I have now attended St Mary's Tremlett for 85 years.

I am thinking of sitting in a different pew one day.

Dolores McDonald

Dear Sir

Some vicars let the organists pick the hymns. Others decide they want to take direct responsibility for the church music themselves.

I have been explaining to Revd Nathan how tricky it is for newcomers to play the organ at St Mary's. And noting how rare organists are round here. And how much they expect to be paid.

I am pleased to say that I will continue to pick the hymns after all.

Maisie Daisie

Dear Sir

I'm not saying that the vicar's sermon was uninteresting last week. But his snoring woke me up halfway through.

Ranulf Bling

Dear Sir

As a churchwarden, I often have some unexpected 'surprises' with respect to church maintenance. But none so great as when I went to drain the water from the font for a baptism, the week after the Pet Service.

Can whoever forgot their piranha please come and retrieve it? I would like to thank Dr Ireland, who removed it from my nose.

Felicity Broadstairs

Dear Sir

Every Wednesday the vicar pops along to our bell-ringing practice and tells us we are very welcome, after ringing on Sunday morning, to stick around for Communion.

Which is very kind. But is he aware that the service time overlaps with the pub being open?

Tim Tang

Dear Sir

I seem to have caused some upset last Sunday.

Revd Nathan, in his 'God of Science' sermon, invited us to wonder at the age of the fossils at the east end of the church.

Turns out he meant the Jurassic sea creatures in the stone walls. I really shouldn't have stared so hard at the choir.

James Dumpling

Dear Sir

Lovely to see the food bank taking place in the church hall every week. Such generosity from the church members. Such a blessing to the parish's poor!

About the poor, however. Some appear to be turning up in cars, and to own mobile phones. When challenged, they say how else could they get a job? Seems to me they aren't trying hard enough to *be* poor.

Marais de Sandeman

Dear Sir

People ask why, against the customs of the church, I live in the Old Vicarage, right in the middle of the parish where I used to be in charge.

The answer is simple. I don't trust the new vicar.

Canon Vyvyan Westclyffe (retired)

Dear Sir

Over the last year, I have come to some realisations about my faith, and my role in the church.

I don't believe in God. I find the vicar's sermons boring and implausible. I don't like church music and I have never enjoyed singing. The occasional use of incense brings on my asthma, and the dampness of the building makes me susceptible to colds.

If I weren't on the prayer, tea and stewarding rotas, I might not even come to church each week.

Mariella Martin

Dear Sir

I was concerned to see a leaflet come through my door advertising the regular services at St Mary's.

If more people start coming to church, we may have trouble parking.

Bradley Hadleigh

SOCIAL LIFE

Dear Sir

I am pleased to inform your readers that once again I will be running the vase stall at the annual church fête. Last year we actually sold a vase, which means we now only have another 97 to sell.

If current rates continue, we expect to sell the last vase in the year 2195.

Billy Bunions

Dear Sir

The period up to Christmas becomes busier every year! Between the Mothers' Union dinner, the Advent carol service, the carol-singing at the Hanged Man Inn, the Nativity, the Christmas carol service – it's a real logjam of activity.

Because of this congestion, the Christmas Fayre will be held in the church hall on 8 May.

Romilly Randers

Dear Sir

When we advertised the 'Children's Advent Workshop', we really meant a craft activity where the children could create nativity sets and do glass painting, to celebrate the coming Christmas season.

I have no idea why everyone turned up with saws, hammers and nails. Totally different kind of workshop.

Rosina Patsey-Tomkinson

Dear Sir

I really don't know what came over me at the fête.

The vicar was so kind to volunteer to be the target to throw wet sponges at. But when I saw the coconut shy, and remembered that awful sermon on 1 Thessalonians, I just lost control.

I hope the bruising, and smell of coconut, go down soon.

Mandy Pandy

Dear Sir

Thanks to the church team for taking part in the annual charity football match against the pub! This year's suspension of the match after 63 minutes was a new record. Two broken ankles and a dislocated shoulder are also an improvement on last year, when Mr Dumpling broke both legs.

Given the average age of the church team was 67, can I suggest dominoes instead next year?

Gavin Drinkswell

Dear Sir

We are cancelling the Ladies' Friendship Group.

We've realised we all hate each other.

Romilly Randers

Dear Sir

When the recent carol service poster advertised 'nibbles with the choir' after the service, I may have misinterpreted it slightly.

Twiglets, peanuts and mini quiches were nothing like as exciting as what I was expecting.

Richard Pendle

Dear Sir

The Civil War Re-creation Society really caused a stir on the village green last week!

I guess you could say that memories run deep. The Arts and Crafts Society have never forgiven the Roundheads for stealing our beautiful painting, *Madonna in the Sunflower Field*, in 1645.

Bad news for Colonel Devereux's Regiment. They were pulling raffia out of their ears for days.

Ranulf Bling

Dear Sir

I remember when we first decided to hold coffee mornings in the church hall. We thought it would be a form of mission. And it has proved very successful. We are open three days a week. And have as many as 50 attendees, who love to discuss Tremlett in the old days and local goings-on.

I attribute our success to the decision we made in 1981 to ban all mention of religion.

Randolph Peranguam

Dear Sir

Thanks to Romilly, who organised last week's training course on conflict resolution.

Such a shame that it ended in a fight.

Felicity Broadstairs

Dear Sir

The annual parish 'Beating the Bounds' was a great joy, as we processed around the fields and along the country lanes around Tremlett.

I am now recovering after being chased by that bull on Naughtie's Farm. Aggie's over her hypothermia from when she fell in the pond. And Romilly's broken leg should set okay.

I'm looking forward to next year already!

Bradley Hadleigh

CHILDREN

Dear Sir

After eighteen years of leading Children's Church, it was time for a break. The effort I had to put in when so few children arrived – some Sundays none at all – meant I called it a day.

The first week of my retirement, there were twelve children in the church. Revd Nathan encouraged them to take an active part in the service.

I have now been asked to take up my old job again. I would like to thank everyone for their many presents of chocolate, gin and money.

Rosina Patsey-Tomkinson

Dear Sir

Since my father is patron of the parish, it seemed only right to drop into Children's Church last week, and check whether the Cholmondeley Nativity Set, donated to the children of the parish in 1904, was still in use.

The Nativity Set was boxed up. In a closed cupboard. Unavailable to the children to play with. An utter insult to my family. I know it is the middle of June, but that is no excuse.

Lady Alicia Cholmondley-Cholmonley

Dear Sir

Okay. It was a mistake for me to provide doughnuts, chocolates and fizzy drinks to the children at Messy Church. I thought they would appreciate a treat and be encouraged to come back next month.

The resultant sugar rush caused them to be surprisingly active and independently minded. I will never forget the look on Miss Patsey-Tomkinson's face as the wooden Noah's Ark set was thrown into the church boiler. And who knew jam doughnuts exploded like that?

Felicity Broadstairs

Dear Sir

Well done to the vicar for allowing children to take a full, active part in the church.

But, if they do a Bible reading, can they be provided with a box to stand on?

Last week I woke up halfway through Henry's reading and thought the lectern was haunted.

Randolph Peranguam

Dear Sir

There are those who say children should have their own church – spending most of the time in the school room, and then coming into the service at the end to show the grown-ups what they have been doing.

But the vicar's experimental All Ages Together service has proved them wrong.

They set fire to his robes with a candle, knocked over the bookcase, and built a wall across the aisle, constructed from hymn books and a couple of choristers they'd kidnapped.

They should never *leave* the school room on Sundays.

Ciara Meringe

THEY SHOULD BE MADE TO GO OUT TO THEIR OWN ACTIVITIES

Dear Sir

Last Sunday a young woman attended church with her baby. Unfortunately, the baby was unsettled and cried for 20 minutes. Some people glared – I believe one or two even tutted. And she left, very upset.

This is very wrong. Young parents should not suffer this kind of ordeal.

They should stay away from church altogether until the children are ten.

Darius D. Mead

Dear Sir

I write to protest about the extravagance of the Church Council. The proposed new toys and carpet for the children's corner could cost as much as £74.22.

My great-uncle gave the church that carpet in 1921. It has years of wear left in it yet.

I therefore have no alternative. I resign as church treasurer.

Norbert Dranesqueezer

Dear Sir

I attended the Tremlett Toddlers' Group last week.

In retrospect, I had no real idea of what I was expecting. But it turned out the place was crawling – often literally – with small children. What is the point of that?

Felicity Broadstairs

Dear Sir

The youth work policy at St Mary's appears to be working. We regularly have between four and eight teenagers attending services.

Some of them are over 6 feet tall, and a couple have tattoos or nose-piercing. Frankly, they are terrifying.

Perhaps we should focus on mission to the elderly?

Ranulf Bling

Dear Sir

On Sunday, we went to church and Rosina, our Sunday School teacher, was ill so me and the other children had to sit in the whole time. We cheered when David beat Goliath. And when Rev Nathan said Jesus was alive, we clapped because that is good.

Why did Mrs Meringe say we had to be quiet? Has no one told her that Jesus is alive?

Grizwold Grommet (age 6½)

Dear Sir

I note that, since I last came to St Mary's, you have installed a new 'children's corner'. Brightly coloured toys, some really engaging books and the dearest little Shaker-style furniture!

I fear that this may attract children. Did nobody think of this?

Bradley Hadleigh

MONEY

Dear Sir

Stewardship Sunday is upon us. The day when the Bishop's enforcer comes down to threaten us with closure if we don't stump up the readies.

If we don't pay enough into the collection, we won't get another vicar when the current one goes. And we won't be able to spend enough money on the building, so it will fall down.

On the bright side, I'll get a lie-in on Sundays.

Mendacity Meadows

Dear Sir

Once again, the vicar has treated us to a sermon on tithing. He mentioned that the Church of England would like us to give 5% of our income to the church – and another 5% to charities and good causes of our choice.

If I were to take Revd Nathan seriously, this would imply I earn £20 per week. I am far better paid than that. Please amend this advice immediately.

Chas 'Charlie' Charkles

Dear Sir

The thermometer in the churchyard, showing the progress of the Steeple Renovation Fund, has been in place so long that English Heritage have listed it.

After 30 years' service, it is in need of maintenance itself. So we have started a 'Thermometer Fund' and put up a smaller thermometer next to it.

Randolph Peranguam

Dear Sir

The vicar is always telling us the church needs more money.

But I got him that paper round and he refused to take it.

Maisie Daisie

Dear Sir

If it's the poor that enter the kingdom of heaven, how come everybody at St Mary's speaks so posh?

Tony Tenor

Dear Sir

Congratulations to the people who contributed to the Bake Sale and Cake Competition. Raised £74. After subtracting the costs of light, heating and prizes, we were able to donate £2.17 to church funds.

Billy Bunions

Dear Sir

Thanks to those who bought items from the Everything for a Pound Sale. We raised £325.49. A great improvement on last year, when it was £213.42.

Fennel Bailey

Dear Sir

Every year we spend more money than is given in offerings. Every year we wonder how we will make it through.

I have told the vicar the obvious way of easing our annual losses: bank robbery.

I've offered him my shotgun and one of Mrs Dumpling's stockings to put on his head. But he says Jesus wouldn't like it.

James Dumpling

Dear Sir

The church should do something about Revd Nathan's wages. We sing 'We have a King who rides a donkey', but we also have a vicar who rides a moped. Better pay for vicars now!

And I notice that the annual Parish Share we pay to the church has gone up 4%. A shocking imposition. Who will join me in a campaign to refuse? Can't pay, won't pay!

Arnold P. Ransome

Dear Sir

Once again, the PCC has – against my advice – voted to spend money on frivolities. Buying chocolate biscuits to eat after Sunday services is a massive luxury and may cost an extra £74.22 per year.

I therefore have no option but to resign as treasurer. Someone else will have to make the savage cuts required to pay for this.

Norbert Dranesqueezer

WORSHIP

Dear Sir

Well done to Revd Nathan for introducing a Taizé service on the third Sunday in the month. Dragging the church into the 1980s!

I will be boycotting it as a nasty modern innovation. But it will be a nice change from boycotting Celtic worship on the first Sunday.

Drenzil Snowflake

Dear Sir

There has been a robed choir at St Mary's since 1874.

Surely some of them should have retired by now?

Billy Bunions

Dear Sir

I attended church for a wedding last Saturday. There were prayers to God, readings from the Bible and a blessing in the name of the Trinity.

Had I known the church was engaging in this kind of shameless Christian propaganda, I would never have been conned into going.

Angela Millways

Dear Sir

The vicar has suspended me from leading prayers in church. Just because, instead of regular confessions, I read out the names of a number of worshippers, and what they needed forgiveness for.

Makes you wonder what he is hiding.

Dr Sandra Ireland

Dear Sir

Every Sunday it's the same from the pulpit – 'God, God, God'. Why can't the vicar mix it up and do some tightrope walking or something? Liven things up a bit.

Randolph Peranguam

Dear Sir

I have been accused of overreacting to the dreadful modern hymns that are inflicted on us. To be fair, I should not have encouraged Junior Church to pour cleaning fluid into the organ, to stop Maisie playing 'Lord of the Dance'.

Ranulf Bling

Dear Sir

People wonder why the choir endure rehearsals in freezing weather, turning out for weddings to sing 'Angels' by Robbie Williams, the vicar's attempts at modern songs, and the constant complaints from the congregation that Elise is out of tune.

Well, we do it because we want to worship God and help others.

And we have a great view of Revd Nathan's bald spot getting that bit bigger each week.

Tony Tenor

Dear Sir

Revd Nathan must restrain his trendy approach to Church of England worship. We are a small, traditional village church. We don't need cutting-edge liturgy.

Take the time of open prayer last week. Everyone was invited to share words from God, or a passage of scripture. Tobias Scrofula decided God was calling him to share the whole of the book of Exodus with us. If the churchwardens had not thrown him out, we would still be there now.

Carla Bonsai

Dear Sir

'Erudite', 'elegant', 'exquisite': three words starting with the same letter – just like the three points in the vicar's sermon on Advent Sunday.

Sadly, that's where the resemblance ends. Pull yourself together, Nathan!

Rob Runes

Dear Sir

Every time I go to church, the vicar has readings that bang on about the poor. Blessed are the poor, look after the poor – orphans and foreigners – that's all we get.

Why can't we have some readings where good things happen to rich people, for a change?

Lady Alicia Cholmondley-Cholmonley

Dear Sir

Choral Evensong is a beautiful English tradition. It is an absolute joy each month: the candlelight, the purity of the choir's voices, the dignity of the Prayer Book.

So. No surprise at the way my sermon, 'You needy brood of whinging vipers', was received.

I'd taken six services. And not eaten all day. And ended up telling you all what I really thought, instead of the sermon I had written.

I *should* apologise.

Revd Nathan

Dear Sir

The vicar used to preach from the pulpit. With the beautiful acoustics in St Mary's, this meant that his sermons were perfectly audible to everyone in the church – including to those of us in the choir.

But he decided he needed to be 'trendy'. Maybe he wanted to be 'down with the kids'. So he started preaching while wandering around the church. And now the choir cannot hear anything he says.

This is a vast improvement. Keep it up!

Tony Tenor

Dear Sir

I would like to apologise for my behaviour at the service with the Archdeacon.

I misheard the service name and thought it was the 'Swearing at', not 'Swearing-in of', churchwardens. I'm afraid I let a whole year of frustration at the state of the memorials go to my head.

Chas 'Charlie' Charkles

Dear Sir

With the introduction of the Psychoactive Substances Bill, I became concerned. The church is full of incense. And what is incense if not something that stimulates the nervous system? I know it stimulates mine.

I felt I had to act before the police appeared in the Trim Valley. I decided I needed to hide the incense in an Aubrey.

I would like to apologise to Aubrey. He has been very forgiving. And explained that what I really should do was put the incense in an aumbry. Different word entirely.

James Dumpling

Dear Sir

Candles are expensive. We use two candles on the altar, two around the altar and two for the acolytes. That's six candles lit every week. It soon adds up.

Yet when I pointed out to the vicar that we are spending £74.22 on candles every year, he said it was money well spent.

I therefore have no alternative but to resign as treasurer.

Norbert Dranesqueezer

COMMITTEES

Dear Sir

I am afraid we must cancel next week's standing committee. We don't have enough chairs.

Romilly Randers

Dear Sir

At last week's Church Council, the vexed subject of the light bulb in the church hall toilet came up. Many wanted the new halogen bulbs, but others thought a compact fluorescent bulb would be cheaper. Mabel reminisced about the good old 100W bulbs that we can no longer use.

Four hours we discussed it, and still no decision. Maybe next month.

Ranulf Bling

Dear Sir

The Mission Committee has once again failed to meet for a whole year. This is because we are busy on the Social Events Committee, the Children's Work Committee, the Finance Committee, the Stewardship Committee and the Church Council.

We have therefore set up the new Committee Overload Committee to see what we can do about too many committees.

Felicity Broadstairs

Dear Sir

Great Tremlett Church Council meetings are known for their length. But the last was exceptional. Lasted so long that there were two births and a retirement party.

James Dumpling

Dear Sir

Thanks to Romilly for her work as the secretary of the Church Council over the last four years. The minutes have been immaculate. It's just some of the hours that have been unbearable.

Revd Nathan

85

Dear Sir

I have been on Tremlett Parochial Church Council for the last 20 years. I have been an active member of the Fundraising Committee and enthusiastically supported the Friday-night bingo and Harvest suppers.

And now I have discovered that something called 'services' happen on Sundays. Why did nobody tell me? I wondered what the bloke in the black shirt was for.

Drenzil Snowflake

Dear Sir

We on the Committee Overload Committee have discovered that there is also a Church Activities Rationalisation Committee doing the same job.

We have therefore started the Duplication of Effort Committee. But it turns out the vicar has also set up a Duplication Task Force.

Felicity Broadstairs

SOCIAL ACTIVITIES

Dear Sir

I must apologise for the trouble I caused in the church hall last week.

I thought it had been hired out to a group of people encouraging the use of Hindu spirituality. Naturally, I ran into the hall, throwing buckets of holy water around, and shouting, 'Evil pagans! God will avenge!'

It transpires that Mrs Dewey, who gave me the information, has a common but maybe not standard pronunciation of 'yoghurt'. The group was making craft fermented milk products, and not practising yoga at all.

Dr Sandra Ireland

Dear Sir

To inform your readers that the new Support Group for people with no sense of direction will be held on the second Friday of the month in the church hall. And the village hall. And in a clump of trees next to the Hanged Man Inn.

And, worryingly, in the mobile library.

Romilly Randers

THE CHURCH YEAR

Dear Sir

Who had the bright idea of giving each child a real candle for Candlemas?

Combined with the amount of hairspray that Rosina uses, this was never going to be a good move. That's the first time I've ever had to wrap someone's head in a choir robe to starve them of oxygen.

Felicity Broadstairs

Dear Sir

Easter Sunday and yet again we had a sermon on the resurrection. The lack of imagination of our clergy is quite remarkable.

And don't get me started on Christmas.

Randolph Peranguam

Dear Sir

Why does the vicar keep telling us that Easter is not over?

All the eggs are eaten. The Christmas puddings are already being sold in Tesco. Of course Easter is over. Get over it.

Rob Runes

Dear Sir

The Harvest Festival! A wonderful reminder of God's fruitful blessings.

Overexcited by Mildew's homemade parsnip wine, I made an expensive bid for the winner of the 'biggest pumpkin' competition. Not having any idea how to cook it, instead I shoved it over my head and ran into the Harvest Messy Church shouting, 'I am the Spirit of the Pumpkin People.'

I hear some children have needed counselling. Could I, by way of amends, offer their parents a bag of frozen pumpkin?

James Dumpling

Dear Sir

I know the vicar believes the Pet Service is part of the church's 'mission'. But what pays for cleaning afterwards? Church funds, that's what. £74.22 this year.

I demanded that the vicar ceases this annual ruining of the 18th-century wooden floor. But he refuses.

I therefore have no alternative but to resign as church treasurer.

Norbert Dranesqueezer

Dear Sir

People worry about interfaith marriages. But it is our Silver Wedding next year, and we have never had a cross word.

My wife's Methodism has never taken an extreme form. However, we have guinea pigs. I always ensure she has no opportunity of sacrificing them and inspecting their entrails on John Wesley's birthday.

Tim Tang

Dear Sir

When the vicar told us that 'all pets are welcome' at the Pet Service, he forgot to say that mine were not.

Barely had I arrived at St Mary's with a couple of swarms of bees when the churchwardens indicated – via a megaphone – that I should leave.

I have not felt so unwelcome since I brought along the tarantulas.

Mendacity Meadows

THE MODERN WORLD

Dear Sir

As well as the website, we now have our own Facebook page for St Mary's Tremlett.

I have ensured that I post a news item to it every day, detailing every activity – however badly attended – in a desperate attempt to make it look like there is some life in the church.

Please could anyone with a Facebook account 'share' the activities to their own timelines, to help with this attempt at deception. I mean mission. Mission.

Romilly Randers

Dear Sir

It is my practice, on dull afternoons, to sit in St Mary's, enjoying the peace and feeling spiritual.

Then last Sunday at six o'clock some people came in and started reading aloud out of a book and singing.

Called themselves 'the congregation'. Who knew this was happening?

Cherry Bassett

Dear Sir

Tried, with no success, to access the new, exciting church so-called Facebook page today. Rubbish. Couldn't find it.

My grandson tells me that this is because I don't have an internet connection. Or a computer. Or a mobile phone.

This is no excuse. The church's social media policy has failed.

Chas 'Charlie' Charkles

Dear Sir

I have 51 fascinating years of temperature records for Tremlett. Yet Romilly claims, 'They're boring and pointless and nobody would read them' and won't upload them to the church website.

She may be missing the point of the internet.

Rob Runes

Dear Sir

A poem, 'Our Neighbours', to celebrate our beautiful Trim
Valley countryside and its fauna:

The hedgehog ambles through the ley
The fieldfare sings in cheerful key
The dormouse wakens from its sleep
The rabbits over tussocks leap
The fox will scurry through the dew
But the tractor smashes them all to goo.
Death, death, death, death.
Death, death, death, death.

Melissa Sparrow (Mrs)

Dear Sir

I hear that the vicar has been tweeting again. I heartily approve.

The more he connects to people through the internet, the less time he will have to mess up his ministry in real life.

Canon Vyvyan Westclyffe (retired)

Dear Sir

My grandson has just logged me on to the new church website. Appalled.

I was expecting to see an archive of all the old magazines, scanned and recorded for a worldwide readership. The church magazine goes back to the 1654 edition, with its headline 'Christmas Fayre cancelled due to Christmas being cancelled'.

Darius D. Mead

Dear Sir

Last month, the vicar married a couple who had been quite publicly living together for the past two years. I realise this kind of thing goes on in big cities like Banbury or Leamington. But in Tremlett? When I was a child they would have been flogged by the pond first.

Dr Sandra Ireland

Dear Sir

The new church magazine cover features a fine picture of the church, standing amongst our ancient and beautiful yew trees.

The previous cover was from a 16th-century wood print, when the yews were much younger, giving a view of the statue of St Myrtle, removed by the Roundheads in 1646.

If you continue with this cover, Cromwell will have won.

Richard Pendle

Dear Sir

Last week a child was baptised whose family are not regular churchgoers. I was surrounded by strangers who didn't understand what was going on.

When our Lord told us to 'make disciples; baptising them', he clearly said we should go *out* to do it. No mention of them suddenly turning up at church and not knowing the hymns or when to kneel.

Romilly Randers

Dear Sir

I note that the new church newsletter has been printed in a Calibri 11-point font on light green paper. Why? The newsletter has been in Times New Roman since 1924, and the vicar has changed things without consultation. This is not the church I grew up in.

Chas 'Charlie' Charkles

Dear Sir

Since the number 91 bus no longer runs into the village on Sundays, I have not been able to make it to church due to lack of transport.

This makes a nice change. Up to now, I've not gone to church because I didn't want to.

Angela Millways

Dear Sir

While I applaud the idea of providing filter coffee instead of the current horrible instant coffee after services, I worry that this may attract new people to church. And then the coffee budget will be impacted.

Keep it vile, keep it quiet – that's my motto.

Bradley Hadleigh

THE CURATE

Dear Sir

I cannot believe that, 20 years after *Dibley*, people are still surprised that our new curate is a woman.

I'm not saying we have to like this fact. But at least we can stop being surprised by it.

Billy Bunions

Dear Sir

The fuss over our new curate, Joanna, takes me back to the days of the old vicar, Giles Dingwall.

Father Dingwall kept goats. You could say he was obsessed with goats. Goats grazed the churchyard. Goats in the vicarage garden. Goats in the vicarage itself. Goats roaming the village green. The village stank of goats.

In Father Dingwall's day, the goat problem was such that nobody went to church because it was full of goats.

But at least he was not a woman.

Dr Sandra Ireland

Dear Sir

I'm encouraged to see Revd Joanna thriving as curate. Still.
A word of warning? She should use her undoubted gifts, but
never be tempted to the over-use of authority. It is a terrible
thing to see a woman being overly assertive in a church that
was, after all, set up by a man.

Could the vicar please call in at the Manor House in the next
week or two? The gutters need clearing.

Lady Alicia Cholmondley-Cholmonley

Dear Sir

Outraged to see Revd Joanna wear red nail varnish at Communion last week.

Our Lord never wore nail varnish at the last supper. Joanna should take note.

Rob Runes

Dear Sir

I fear that, when Revd Joanna is fully trained and gets her own church, she may be terribly overstretched.

How can she run a parish, look after her children and still do all the housework and cook for her husband?

The baking will suffer, believe me.

Ciara Meringe

Dear Sir

I yield to no one in my admiration for our curate, Father Joanna. He has fitted in well, with his enthusiasm, obvious love of God and oddly high voice.

Obviously, we also love Joanna's family. But Joanna's wife, Ronald, worries me. Not only does she have a beard and work as a builder, but she is useless at making jam.

Something is wrong.

Chas 'Charlie' Charkles

Dear Sir

I thoroughly approve of Revd Joanna's commitment to inter-faith dialogue. An open, charitable, welcoming faith is surely one that is self-confident and prepared to learn from others.

But a replica Stonehenge in the front garden? Maybe she has gone a little too far?

Rosina Patsey-Tomkinson

Dear Sir

Concerning the debate about what to call the curate, if we can't call her 'Father'. People have suggested 'Reverend', 'Mother' or 'Sister'. Personally, I just call her 'Matron'. She doesn't like it, but it makes me feel very comfortable.

James Dumpling

Dear Sir

Every Sunday the curate follows me home, eats dinner, sits in the living room and waits until *Downton Abbey* is on. Then she drinks my gin and abuses the characters for being 'posh'.

Some would say she's just being overly keen in pastoral matters, but it makes me feel uncomfortable. And I don't care if she is my wife.

(*Name withheld*)

Dear Sir

So the new curate is complaining about her house. It seems the unheated two-bedroomed cottage is not suitable for her, her husband and their four children.

This modern generation! When I was a curate, I lived in a tent in the vicar's garden. Never did me any harm. Although I did lose my first wife in the cold winter of '63.

Canon Vyvyan Westclyffe (retired)

THE BUILDING

Dear Sir

I hear the vicar wishes to move the light switch in the church from the north wall to the east door – because 'that's where we come in and we won't need to use a torch'.

I have protested to English Heritage, the Council and the Pope. And they all told me they didn't care. I went to St Mary's once when I was nine and I don't see why it should change now.

Marvis Dripping

Dear Sir

It is wonderful that our pretty graveyard is still in use and will be for many decades to come. And Jeb works so hard at keeping the place trim and neat.

But when he has a job to do, it would be much better if he could do it at the weekend, not after work in the dark. He terrified poor Mr James, climbing out the newly dug grave like that.

Felicity Broadstairs

Dear Sir

I'm objecting to the vicar's plans to replace the church steps with a slope, to allow wheelchair users easy access.

This is an undesirable change to the architecture. It also implies Revd Nathan doesn't have faith in his own prayer ministry.

Chas 'Charlie' Charkles

Dear Sir

The vicar is talking about removing some of the pews from St Mary's to 'create a more flexible worship space'. Disgraceful!

The church should be preserved for future generations. This is my family church – the one that has stood for centuries. We love it just as it is.

One day I may even come in and have a look round.

Roland Yoland

Dear Sir

I object to the plans to put toilets and a kitchen into the space beneath the bell tower.

When 'caught short', we used to have to run out of the building and perform necessary functions behind the wall in Church Lane. And if we wanted a drink in church, we had to bring our own beer.

The new generation has gone soft.

James Dumpling

Dear Sir

Turned up to the Fabric Committee last week and they just talked about the building.

I'd lugged my sewing machine all the way to the church hall for nothing.

Ciara Meringe

Dear Sir

All this talk of lead thieves. I do something about it, and I just get complaints.

Yes, the gentleman was left dangling from the gutter, after I pushed his ladder over. But he wasn't there long. When I poked him with the Scouts' flag, he soon fell off.

Maisie Daisie

Dear Sir

Last Sunday I noticed that the ladies washing up after the post-service coffee were not using my Aunt Annie's 'Footprints' tea towel. She bequeathed that towel 25 years ago.

Until my aunt's tea towel is reinstated, I will be boycotting the church hall.

Marais de Sandeman

Dear Sir

I have spent the afternoon in the church with my laser measuring device, and there is no doubt. At some point in the last twelve months, the lectern has been moved at least nine inches to the right, as viewed from the congregational point of view. When did the Church Council vote for this?

Chas 'Charlie' Charkles

Dear Sir

There is a hole in the roof, letting in water directly above the rear right-hand pew. Whenever I speak to the churchwardens, they say it will be expensive to fix and we need to get three estimates.

This is taking for ever. Some Sunday mornings I go home soaked.

I'm seriously considering sitting in another pew.

Mandy Pandy

THE REPOINTING DOES MAKE IT LOOK A LOT BETTER

Dear Sir

While polishing the candlesticks in church last week, I spent too much time in the cupboard where we keep the polish, cleaning sprays and incense. As a result, I have spent three weeks convinced I am a leather-bound edition of *Hymns Ancient and Modern*.

If anyone needs me, I will be stacked in the shelves.

James Dumpling

Dear Sir

The temperature in church on Christmas Eve was −1.5°C. This was the coldest service since January 1979, when ice formed on the font and a baptism had to be abandoned.

Rob Runes

Dear Sir

It's wonderful to take the children from Tremlett School around St Mary's. It introduces them to the history of the village and helps them to be part of our living tradition.

But last week the children were terrified by a hideous gargoyle. It has put them right off the church.

Can you please ask Mr Dumpling not to sleep in the pews during the day?

Fennel Bailey

CHRISTMAS

Dear Sir

It is a joy, every Christmas Fayre, to try out the exciting new chutneys and jams that have been produced.

This year I was, however, unwise enough to make a cheese toastie with Mrs Braybrooke's strawberry and chilli chutney. I hope to be allowed out of the house by Easter.

James Dumpling

Dear Sir

After complaints that last year's Midnight Mass 'went on too late', this year's service will start at 8.00 pm. It may not genuinely be the full Midnight Mass experience, but at least everyone will get their cocoa on time.

Revd Nathan

Dear Sir

It's lovely the children all want to be in the Nativity play, but some of the animals in the stable were a bit unlikely this year.

Ox and ass, fine. Camel, sheep and horse – okay. But penguins, meerkats and wallabies? Not only are they not in the Gospels, they don't even live in the Holy Land. Little Delroy looked lovely in his costume, but an alien? In Bethlehem?

Billy Bunions

RELUCTANT SHEEP

SEVERAL SANTAS

FAIRY GODMOTHER

SUPERMAN

LOST ANGEL

ESCAPED DONKEY

THE SEVEN WISE MEN

DARTH VADER

Dear Sir

I know he likes to get into the Christmas spirit, but please can Revd Nathan not wear that festive Rudolph jumper with the glowing nose this year? Or, at least, not during Midnight Mass.

Romilly Randers

Dear Sir

Every Christmas the church brings us 'Beer and Carols' at the Hanged Man Inn.

The beer is fine, but why do they have to spoil it with the carols?

Angela Millways

Dear Sir

A dreadful performance by young Esme Dermer as the Virgin Mary at this year's Nativity play. Lacking depth and nuance – and failing to project the aura of saintliness we expect in the part.

Perhaps next Christmas the vicar should follow the evidence of his eyes and ears – and not his evident attraction to Esme's mother – and cast my little Evangelina in the role she was born to.

Maisie Daisie

Dear Sir

I walked past the church this morning, and saw that somebody has hung up a series of letters spelling out 'MERRY CHRIST'. This is heresy. Our Lord was 'a man of sorrows and acquainted with grief'. This is the kind of thing you expect to see when the church has sold out to the people who sing 'One More Step Along the World I Go'.

Dolores McDonald

Dear Sir

Since the vicar is very good at asking God for things, can he ask for snow this Christmas? It would make it really great. And could he ask God to let Santa know I'd like a reindeer? Not a toy one.

Grizwold Grommet (age 6½)

Dear Sir

What a joy once again to attend the Nativity service at St Mary's. I often say to myself that I should attend church more frequently the rest of the year. But I came along once in Lent and it was really miserable. Not even any tinsel.

See you next Christmas.

Jasmine Jones

Dear Sir

Saw the Nativity Play. What was that about?

Why did the children of the parish think anybody would be interested in the so-called 'Christmas Story'? The Son of God being born in a stable? Who would believe that? Where was Santa?

When I started booing, the churchwardens held my elbows very tightly as they led me out. Left me with a slight bruise. Ruined my Christmas. Season of goodwill? I don't think so.

Richard Pendle

Dear Sir

At the Christmas Eve Nativity service, I brought up with the vicar the need to repoint the north wall.

He told me that he was 'quite busy with four more services' and asked if we could meet at a more suitable time.

I went round after lunch the following day. And was told that he was unavailable as he was 'asleep in his chair'. What a lack of commitment!

Dr Sandra Ireland

Dear Sir

I walked past the church again this evening, and see that somebody has hung up three more letters. The sign now reads 'MERRY CHRISTMAS'. Thank you for responding to my first letter so quickly.

Dolores McDonald

Dear Sir

The most wonderful time of the year! I have composed
a poem to celebrate it – 'Christmas':

The ringers ring in the Nativity.
The old church is full of activity.
The carollers sing the age-old tale.
Then out in the orchard they cry, 'Wassail'!
The joy and the peace between friend and friend.
But soon all this happiness comes to an end.
Death, death, death, death.
Death, death, death, death.

Melissa Sparrow (Mrs)

Dear Sir

As usual I attended the Christmas morning service. Children receiving presents that had nothing to do with the birth of our Lord. Hungover choristers wincing as they hit the high notes. Revd Joanna preaching a four-minute sermon, so she could get back to the turkey.

And in the middle of it all, a tiny doll in a plastic crib, representing the maker of all, come to earth as a baby.

We should do it every year.

Ranulf Bling

Transforming lives and communities

Christian growth and understanding of the Bible

Resourcing individuals, groups and leaders in churches for their own spiritual journey and for their ministry

Church outreach in the local community

Offering three programmes that churches are embracing to great effect as they seek to engage with their local communities and transform lives

Teaching Christianity in primary schools

Working with children and teachers to explore Christianity creatively and confidently

Children's and family ministry

Working with churches and families to explore Christianity creatively and bring the Bible alive

Visit **brf.org.uk** for more information on BRF's work
Review this book on Twitter using **#BRFconnect**

brf.org.uk

The Bible Reading Fellowship (BRF) is a Registered Charity (No. 233280)